Love & Psychosis

A Poetry Collection

Mariah Stockdale

ISBN
EBOOK: 978-1-971141-60-2
PAPERBACK: 978-1-971141-61-9
HARDCOVER: 978-1-971141-62-6

Dedication

To my loved ones, thank you for loving me

To the reader, thank you for choosing me

About The Author

Mariah Stockdale is a 31-year-old writer from Nova Scotia. She is a mom of two who has been recovering from psychosis, and riddled with social anxiety, she strives to get up every day and do her best, whatever that may look like that day.

Foreword

This is a collection of poems I started writing when I was in the hospital with psychosis. These poems are timestamps of the journey to recovery and self-improvement, the ups and downs, and everything in between. My hope is that you will relate to some poems in some way throughout your reading. If I can help someone by sharing my words, I've done good.

TABLE OF CONTENTS

Page Blank Left Intentionally

March 11, 2023 – My Worst Days

On my worst days, I couldn't recognize myself

On my worst days, I wanted to be somewhere else

On my worst days, I couldn't control my feelings

Cause I never really learned how

On my worst days, I couldn't hear the help

On my worst days, I was drowning in my doubts

On my worst days, I couldn't see without the blur

Cause I was dazed and not one with the world

On my worst days, "I'm not worth it" is all I said

On my worst days, I just wanted to stay in bed

On my worst days, I screamed as loud as I could

Cause I thought that's how I would be heard

On my worst day, I couldn't keep it together

On my worst day, I fell harder than ever

On my worst day, I hated myself

Cause I never had the chance to grow for myself

Yearning For you – 03/13/2023

In the middle of the night

I can't seem to sleep

There's someone on my mind

Someone I wish to keep

But can I keep them?

Do they want me?

It's so hard to tell

Is it meant to be?

They were the best to come

The best thing I ever called mine

Treacherous was the slope

But I guess I'll be fine

If I could know the answers

If I knew their heart was mine

I'd call them up and tell them

They have mine till the end of time

Time To Heal - March 2023

It's time to heal for me

At least that's what they say

But how can you trust someone

Or are they here for the pay

It's hard to accept the help

When it's something you fought to have

Trying to accept the help feels wrong

Why does getting help feel so bad

I wish I weren't scared of the professionals

I wish I knew they meant well

Even though that's what they're here for

It feels like an unbelievable spell

The time will come when you aren't scared

The help you're accepting is going to get you there

Love Yourself

Do you need love, or should you love alone?

It always gets lonely when you sit up on the throne

But the wrong person sitting next to you

Causes more damage than anything else will do

So, what do you do when you don't know?

What's the right answer? Which sign is right?

How can you trust that it's more than just lust?

The hurting ones love the way you love them

You'd give your love to those who need it

But would they really appreciate it?

Or would they take the lessons and walk away

Why can't you find someone to water you that way?

My Babies Are My World - 03/18/2023

If I could be anywhere

I'd be with my babies

I'd hold them for a while

My little man and little lady

I miss making them lunch

Or getting them ready

An adventure for the bunch

Just keep moving steady

One day you'll get there

It just takes time

Remember to stop and take in the air

In the end, you'll be fine

Keep holding on to optimism

It's the one thing keeping you going

This place is lacking the love

That you're so used to showing

I Am Made Up Of

I

Am

Made

Up entirely

Of silly songs

& Weird emotions

You can push through

The darkness if you try

But sometimes the darkness

Will swallow a person whole

Past, Present, Future – 04/29/2023

You wouldn't have such troubles

If you listened to yourself

You shouldn't be doubting yourself

Everyone needs a little bit of help

Push right through like you always do

The negative thoughts you keep inside

Are the things that hold you back in life

You Don't Need To Lie

You don't need to lie

You don't have to hide

To protect yourself from awful guys

Be trusting when they show their worth

Light conversation will save you from hurt

Don't conform to what they want

It will leave you filled with haunt

Regret the way you tried to save yourself

But don't put yourself back on the shelf

Do You Really Want To Know Where I Was April 29th?

April 29, 2022, I was screaming, "I don't know what to do"

April 29, 2023, I said, "I want to get better for me and you"

In 2022, I was exhausted from emotions I bottled

In 2023, I released the emotions at full throttle

In 2022, I was unraveling at every seam

In 2023, I wanted to sew up all the open seams

In 2022, my adventure day went awry

In 2023, I wanted to figure out the reasons why

On April 29th of 2024

I hope to open a new door

Momma bear – 03/15/2023

A heart made of gold

Til you mess with my babies

Don't tell me I'm crazy

I'm a momma bear

They are my world

I'd do anything for them

Within my limits, of course

Still a momma bear

No parent is perfect

They all make mistakes

That doesn't always mean

Someone should take their place

I'm a momma bear

Don't come for my cubs

They keep me going

Even when darkness overshadows light

My kids will have better than me

They will see that I can show them better

My patience is being tested

When I see them as often as the weather

Don't fuck with my babies

Don't get in my way

Momma bear will come out

And she doesn't want to play

No time for this bullshit

You have to get better for them

It's hard when you're away from them

Every road bump feels like an intentional hit

I don't want to blow my top

But how could I not?

The one way I feel connected to them

Is in the hands of someone else

This place feels like hell, but it will lead me to heaven if I
just sit still

04/29/2023 - Many Things I've Yet To Learn

So many things I've yet to learn

Freedom from my mind is what I yearn

Paranoia fills me, and my wandering mind

Wish I could shut the thoughts off sometimes

Finding something new to learn would probably help

So many options, but what's best for myself?

Thoughts come back in a moment's chance

"They're out to get me" from a stranger's long glance

How can you learn with unreasonable fear

That danger is lurking or standing near

I must push through like I always do

Find ways to help become the new you

Give yourself a chance and plan out your day

Stick to it, work hard, and don't go astray

Nobody's perfect, and everyone stumbles

You don't need to die because of your tumbles

05/10/2023 – Day Hospital

First day of a new program

Time to figure out who I am

Remember a time when I felt free

A happy-go-lucky kind of me

Not sure what lies in store

I'll find out when I walk through the doors

Trying To Love My Body

Trying to love my body

With the newly gained weight

At least I finally got some

Tell myself, "I look great"

But my words aren't that convincing

Having a hard time trying to believe

I'm still as good as I once was

My old looks are something I grieve

Everything I wear

Seems to be too small

Pants, shirts, anything I own

Jump and shimmy into it all

06/12/2023 – I Went Insane

I went insane

I lost my brain

All my strength was hindered by my pain

Please stay, don't leave

While I build a better me

A better mom, a better friend

The kind you keep to the very end

I want to laugh

I want to dance

I want to give love another chance

I want to build a better past

No more living in a cast

07/??/2023- Kisses And Cuddles

Kisses and cuddles

Hugs of love

The kind of love I'm dreaming of

Handpicked flowers

Dandelion showers

Seeds fluttering through the air

Cheesy gestures

Romantic pleasures

Show me how you care

Listening ears

Want you here

My love for you won't disappear

I Couldn't Get A Cuddle

I couldn't get a cuddle

I couldn't get hugs

All I ever asked for was to be loved

Show me you love me, don't just say it

Until it disappears completely

Finally, I breathed while I was drowning

Left on my own to fight alone

Raising our kids by myself

Not the way I wanted it to be

But the kids and I deserve better

No half-assed "Love"

Won't be tolerated anymore

I Can't Believe I Called That Love

I can't believe I called that love

When we weren't even friends

Just two people co-existing

Barely sleeping in the same bed

In the same bed without sleeping

I can't believe I called that love

When there were times, I begged for a hug

Just to wrap my arms around a statue

Wanting to cuddle

End up in a self-soothing huddle

I can't believe I called that love

Struggling to communicate and compromise

The ultimate results end in demise

Doesn't matter if I'm mean or nice

Silence and shoulders cold as ice

I wish I left sooner, but now I know

That wasn't what I call love

Idk What You're Looking For

I don't know what you're looking for

But I know it's not me

But that doesn't mean

I haven't pondered the possibility

Playing "what if" in fantasy land

What's it like to have your hand?

12/09/2023 – Thank You to My Body

Thank you to my body

Always going strong

Even when the fuel was low

You didn't let go

Thank you to my body

For never giving up

Holding on to something

When I felt like nothing

Thank you to my body

For every breath you breathe

Even when it's filled with smoke

You never quit on me

Thank you to my body

For restoring my life quality

A new path of thinking

New opportunities mending

Thank you to my body

For having the strength

To survive in the dark

Even when things are looking stark

12/09/2023 – Thank You For Loving Me

Thank you for loving me

You're the only man I see

I appreciate you

And the things you do

I love it when we cuddle

My favourite person to snuggle

Going for walks with you

Something I enjoy to do

Always valuing our time

Thankful to have you as mine

Wonder where we'll go

Time will reveal what we don't know

12/09/2023 – Energy Is Fading

My energy is fading

I'm trying to get it done

It's kind of hard when I'm the only one

My spirit is tired

Fighting through the days

Is there an easier way?

My creativity is dying

Confused about what to do next

Always trying to write the perfect text

Where is my muchness?

What happened to me?

What is it in me that you see

12/14/2023 - Thank You for Being There

Thank you for being there

No matter what I look like or wear

Whether I have short or long hair

I'm sorry if I gave you a scare

Thank you for being here

For always staying near

For lending a listening ear

Ignoring all my fears

Thank you for being a friend

Even on days I don't hit send

Weather far away or around the bend

Sticking it out to the end

12 Months of Us – 12/??/2023

Twelve months of us have come and gone

Surprisingly, it doesn't feel that long

Every month, a building block to where we are

Friends finding love in each other's arms

12/??/2023 – A Year Has Come and Gone

A year has come and gone

There were things that went wrong

And things that went right

Winning what seemed to be a losing fight

Slowly but surely at my pace

No more hiding behind a face

Crawling out of a dark space

Feeling like I'm losing a race

Give me a saving grace

You don't want to have a taste

Building myself from the ground

Finally coming around

I'm the kind of girl

That likes to wear a ring

To say that I'm taken

Not looking for anything

I'm the kind of girl

That's loyal and true

Don't need to question

My love is all for you

I'm the kind of girl

That doesn't ask for much

My favourite thing is

A warm, embracing touch

I'm the kind of girl

That cares about your health

Who wants to enhance your life

Who doesn't care about wealth

02/???2024 – Thank You For Caring

Thank you for caring

Actually giving a damn

Turns out the woods

Was a good place to find a man

Better than I imagined

Better than I could have planned

You spoil us with love

You fit like a glove

Handsome and handy

Isn't that dandy

02/27/2024 — Drop-In

She called him just a drop in

But he's taken out my trash

I'm pretty sure a drop in

Would only want to smash

She called him just a drop in

But he's cleaned almost every room

Pretty sure a drop in

Wouldn't pick up the vacuum

She called him just a drop in

But he puts the groceries away

Pretty sure a drop in

Wouldn't be coming every day

She called him just a drop in

But he cooks us food

Pretty sure a drop in

Wouldn't be able to tell my mood

She said he's just a drop in

But he puts the kids to bed

Pretty sure a drop in

Would only want some head

She said he's just a drop in

But he has a set of keys

And I wouldn't let a drop in

Randomly drop in on me

02/26/2024 - Psychosis

The world is out to get me

Distrusting family and friends

The universe is full of signs

Voices in my head

Nobody's who they say they are

Scared of every blue passing car

Nobody listens, nobody cares

I'll be safe if I cut my hair

Do they want me dead or want me alive?

Is the end coming in this ambulance ride?

Are they poisoning the food?

Spinning the wheel of moods

Feel like something is crawling under my skin

Escaping is a challenge I'm going to win

Should I stay or should I run?

Some days were kind of fun

In the woods, I found someone

If we get a room, my life is done

Are you my killer or my lover?

To join the gang, you killed your mother

Mysterious bottle, I didn't smash

Before I threw it in the trash

Thinking I'm on onlyfans

Is this part of the master plan?

2/??/2024 - Mental Health Kicked My Ass

Mental health kicked my ass

Shattered me like a piece of glass

A test or wave to pass

Hunting me by the mass

My choices led me there

Worrying about what I wear

How many eyes are watching me?

How many want me to be free?

Free of my mind

Free of their kind

Freedom from the fear

Voices I hear

Are you my dear?

Will you show up here?

Robots replaced the kids

I really lost my lid

Looking for a sign

I'm running out of time

I have to take these meds

Should I call the feds?

Is it all in my head?

Or real and I'm dead

03/??/2024 — Where Is The Faith

Where is the faith?

That I'll make the right choice

When I make a decision

You will hear my voice

I'm not incapable

Of knowing what's right

No room to argue

No room to fight

How do they know

What's the right move

They're not living my life

They're throwing off my groove

Do they want me to be happy?

Do they want me to be sad?

Why is it that some people

Search for anything negative or bad

Find a reason to complain

Only see things their way

You can't please these people

So don't let them ruin your day

03/23/2024 – Kids Are Kids

Kids are kids

They're going to be loud

Let them laugh

Let them be proud

Allow them to feel

The emotions they have

Show them how to heal

From what makes them sad

Love it when they smile

Love it when they play

Always give you a hug

No matter what kind of day

You are their rock

They are your world

Always cherish them

Your little boy and girl

03/??/2024 – Life Is Looking Better

Life is looking better

I'm on a different path

And I wouldn't be able to do it

Without my other half

I found him in the woods

I found a perfect gem

I had exes, but like a spell

He made me forget about them

I thought he was going to flee

When "I love you" spilled out of me

Something made him say

"I miss her" while I was away

The day came, he finally messaged me back

My heart pounding in overdrive, under attack

Could this really be happening to me?

So many thoughts, which ones to believe?

Welcome to the present day

Helping me grow along the way

03/??/2024 – I Found A Man

I found a man

That stopped me

In my tracks

Changed my plans

To risk something new

Wasn't sure about

The outcome of my choice

A gamble nonetheless

But in the end

It turned out for the best

He gives me his time

Cooks like a chef

Cleans up the house

Helps with the kids

Everything I've wanted

And more besides

I hope he's just as happy

And doesn't see an end

I wouldn't want to lose

My best friend

My favourite person

My loving man

A Self-Proclaimed Poet

A self-proclaimed poet

Built from a shattered heart

Not the best-selling type

But an honest one to start

Hoping to grip onto you

Feel it deep within your soul

A creative string of words

Like they know they have a role

Finding the words for the perfect line

Comes easy for some like me

With days of defeat, saying this is fine

Accepting whatever the line may be

Leaving it up to fate

To express the right emotions

Happy, sad, mad, glad, love, and hate

Inspirations as you decorate the page

Words into lines flowing with rage

Only the reader can decide

Find a favourite poem of mine

Show it to everyone

And read it from time to time

05/??/2024 – Cannabinoid Hyperemesis Syndrome

The waves of nausea are capsizing

Vomit crashing in the bowl

Abdominal cramps galore

Idk if I can handle much more

Hot baths that turn the room into a sauna

To help ease the nausea

Dehydration is almost guaranteed

Needing fluids through IV

Good luck keeping anything down

Praying to keep Zofran in my belly

Counting down until it's ready

Little sips, little bites

Is this all I'll eat tonight?

Seems like an endless fight

Craving to smoke a bowl or joint

But it only prolongs recovery

So, I suffer from withdrawal

In hopes of getting better fast

I want to feel okay when I go to class

04/??/2024 - It's 2024

It's 2024

So many doors

Which to choose?

It's up to you

Should I get my GED?

I know that'd be good for me

26/30 on the Wonderlic exam

Becoming a nail tech is the plan

To make others feel beautiful

Comforting the anxiety of people

No natter nails

The dream sets sail

Accept times you may fail

Lessons learned into the pail

05/15/2024 – Poetry Is More Than just a Rhyme

Poetry is more than just a rhyme

Poetry is considered story time

A fun way to get your point across

Some pieces make you feel less lost

Some short, others long

Some turn into a little song

Full of emotion, full of pride

Taking you on an adventurous ride

Spill your heart, empty your brain

Freedom is what you'll gain

They could be happy, they can be sad

In order to have good ones, you have to have bad

Some people like them, some people don't

It doesn't matter who will and who won't

So, grab a pen and a piece of paper

Write some memories to look at later

05/28/2024 – I Start Again

And so, I start again

Eating and cleaning

Making routines again

Keeping up with daily chores

Try not to eat calories galore

Sleep at appropriate times

Everything is a balancing line

Started at the lowest low

All I can do now is grow

Watch me as I evolve

The issues I resolve

The independence that I need

So, I can be freed

Depends on me

Just wait and see

06/??/2024 – Together We Stand

Together we stand

Stronger than Iron Man

Darling, you're so grand

Take me by the hand

Baby, I love you

Only you will do

I know you feel it too

Even when our brains are stew

Let's go and run away

Save our stress for another day

Our demons we'll slay

'Forcing them into the grey

Our relationship is strong

For the most part, we get along

Smoking together from the bong

Think of you in every love song

06/19/2026 – I Don't Want You to Write

I don't want you to write poems

Because I want to go outside

I want to play on the swings

And play seek and hide

Little does she know

Each time I write a poem

It expresses how I feel

A collection I'm trying to build

Put them in a book to make it feel real

Topics about love and psychosis

The things I'm going through

You're too young to understand now

But one day it will all make sense to you

You might be a poet, and then you'll understand

"Just 5 more minutes while it's still in my head"

Even if you don't become a poet

I hope you like my poems

Remember me in a special way

Everyone knows we all die one day

07/12/2024 – Welcome To July

Welcome to July

Struggling to get by

Can't get out of my own way

No motivation for me today

So many things I have to do

All I want is cuddles with you

Maybe it will help me recharge

My to-do list is quite large

Too overwhelmed to do all the things

To feel a burst of happy, I buy rings

Its second best compared to him

A call, text, or glimpse is a win

Erratic spending, a sign of decline

Tell myself and others, "It's okay, I'm fine"

Don't want to go to the hospital again

So, I do what I can to rein myself in

V4w 4

I'm trying to write a poem

But nothing seems just right

I don't know what the issue is

Or why it seems like a fight

Maybe it's the syllables

Maybe it doesn't rhyme

Where'd I put my flow?

It's hiding well this time

I'm off my meds again

That could be the cause

Each time I write a line

I take a long pause

I hope to get it back

My ability to compose

Create something good

Just wait I suppose

09/??/2024 – I Once Was So Great

I once was so great

I was proud of who I was

Now I'm subpar at best

I don't like the me that I am

I could see how happy I made others

By their smile when I walked in the room

The greetings are dull now, like a worn-out pencil

Merely existing because a new one hasn't come yet

Strangers would comment on my happy kids

Acknowledge the smile on their faces

Tell me I'm doing good, they used to anyways

Until one day they're telling me I don't want to die

And maybe they were right, maybe they were wrong

How I felt was driving me insane, would they feel that way, too?

Had it been the other way around, I'd do the same thing

Maybe they were right about everything.

Strange

09/??/2024 – Going to Lose My Mind

I'm going to lose my mind

Tired of yelling all the time

Repeating myself like a broken record

"Hands are for helping, not hurting"

"First time listening, ears please"

"Pick up your mess you made"

"Leave the kittens alone, let them come to you"

"No stomping, don't push, stop screaming"

I feel like I'm going mad

Maybe even insane

09/??/2024 – Thankful for The Love I Found

I'm so thankful for the love I found

Hearing his voice is a relaxing sound

Without him, I don't know what I'd do

Who would I tell my anxieties to

The safety plan is lifted

I can feel my mood shifted

My baby can finally come back home

And I won't feel so alone

I'm ready to go back on family adventures

Hopefully, through all types of temperatures

09/18/2024 – Like To Write

I like to write poems

To express what's on my mind

Sometimes it's a struggle

Others come in no time

I like to write poems

To procrastinate throughout the day

Find something to write about

Or take my stresses away

I like to write poems

About love and life

And things I'm going through

Things that cut like a knife

I like to write poems

It's therapeutic for me

Maybe I'll publish a book

I guess we'll wait and see

09/??/2024 – Feel Like a Failure

I feel like a failure

Like I'm not doing my best

I feel like I could do better

But first, maybe I should rest

Maybe I'm too hard on myself

That's easy for me to do

When all is said and done

I hope to do right by you

09/20/2024 – Don't Feel Good

I don't feel good

I feel like hurling

Excess saliva building

My stomach just-a-twirling

I don't feel good

So, I get in a hot shower

The same glands control nausea

Give me temperature-regulating power

I don't feel good

And it's been that way for a while

I just want to get better

So, I can go back to having a smile

10/03/2024 – Michaela's Poem

She lives far away

But our friendship is close

Might not talk every day

But I love her the most

She's so smart

And a great mom too

She's got a spot in my heart

Without her, I don't know what I'd do

She survived my psychosis

What a wild time

She loved me when I was atrocious

My spirit covered in grime

She's the peanut butter to my jam

The trees on my land

She's the glaze on my ham

The fingers on my hand

10/12/2024 – Tortured Poet

Tortured poet

Tell me please

What I have to do

To be set free

Should I cry

Should I write

Put up a fight

Gaze into sunlight

Tortured poet

Hear me out

You must find

What life's about

Finding a love

That's pure and true

Having a home

To go back to

Tortured poet

Hear my plea

It might be hard

Please don't leave

10/??/2024 – My Love Is Like Roots on A Tree

My love for you is like roots on a tree

Spreading out, growing strong and rapidly

I love you more than all my fears

When you must leave, it brings me to tears

I love you like I love my health

Holding on no matter what cards have been dealt

I love working together to make some food

Or make spicy videos when we're in the mood

Working together to get the house clean

You're the best love I've ever seen

10/??/2024 – I Was a Sparkler You Lit in The Middle of The Night

I was a sparkler you lit in the middle of the night

You enjoyed my light until it dimmed to a single flame

Eventually burning out

And once my flame finally burned out

You search for someone brighter

Only to find I'm the brightest you've seen

You couldn't replace little old me

Yes, my light was beautiful to look at

But it also provided warmth

Now that your light show is over

You're left feeling cold

Wishing you had someone like me to hold

10/24/2024 – My Love Is Intense

I like to think my love is intense

Overwhelmed by the feeling of being loved

I like to think there's something different

About the way that I love others

Something in a special kind of way

Something that makes them want to love me

But never taking the time to do so

Or understanding how my brain works

Or learning my love language

I felt depleted when trying to stay

But I know when to walk away

Once I've done everything to make it work

And I'm left questioning and broken

That's when I walk away from it all

I love with all I have to offer

I don't give up easy, but when I do

It's not me, it's you

10/??/2024 – All That You Do

Thank you for all that you do

Even if you think it's not much

No one has ever treated me like you

10/??/2024 – I Love You and I Need You

I love you

And I need you

Don't know what I'd do

If I didn't have you

You give me all the kisses

I'll always be your missus

Even if you're full of ridges

I want to pass your quizzes

I want you to have my heart

I hate when we're apart

We're flying like a dart

Put a ring in the cart

10/??/2024 – Thank You for Loving Me

Thank you for loving me

And choosing to be with me

For always spending time with me

No matter how short, no matter how long

Thankful you make time for me at all

11/??/2024 – I Can't Believe It

I can't believe the DISRESPECT

From Sackville Elementary School

Asking vets to wear civilian clothes

That's so not cool

How do you do that

To the people who made you free

Risked their lives by going to war

A war we were blessed not to see

On Canadian soil, we live free

No active wars for us to hide

Free to be you, live how you want

Not being forced to pick a side

They came to Canada to flee

From their war-torn homes

Trauma-filled minds everywhere

Not just them alone

11/??/2024 – In A Slump

I'm in a slump

Feel like a dump

Don't want to get up

Don't want to fill my cup

I just want to sleep all day

Don't want to go out to play

Eat it all or nothing at all

These are signs of an inevitable fall

Body feels heavy, and can barely move

When I do, it feels like I have extra weight too

Speaking of weight, I've grown in size

Much more and faster than I realize

11/21/2024 – Empty

I feel empty

Like I'm just a shell

I don't always feel this way

It's just a dark spell

I don't want to get up

Just lie here and not move

I want to become couch rot

I just want to hit snooze

Part of me thinks

I need a hospital stay

To recover fully

While I swim through the grey

12/01/2024 – December Is Here

Oh my, December is here

As always, I'm missing my Christmas cheer

Arguments are what I fear

Will it be different for me this year

Will the kids be happy with what they get

Or will this be a year they forget

12/??/2024 – The Dreaded Day Has Come

The dreaded day has come

Tomorrow, I quit smoking weed

It's for a good cause

I know it's what I need

I know why I'm doing this

So, I will succeed in school

It's not a forever thing

I plan to smoke again

I just hope I won't be too crabby

And avoid all the moods

12/02/2024 – Look At Her

Look at her hair, perfectly wild

Her eyes glitter and gleam like a child

She always says outrageous things

Hands covered with glitter and rings

She loves to use her fountain pen

Loves Taylor Swift since way back when

She captivates you with a single poem

The kind of love that feels like home

She likes to give big squeezy hugs

Drink coffee from her favourite mug

Talk it out when times get rough

Convince you to stay when you've had enough

Tell you that life's better with you here

Wise, with awesome listening ears

The kind of girl you want as a friend

One to keep around until the very end

12/18/2024 – A Baby Is Coming

A baby is coming

It's going to be cute

My brother helped make it

So it will be wild too

A baby is coming

Is it going to be a boy

Wonder if it'll be a girl

Either way, welcome to the world

A baby is coming

It's due in the spring

Maybe before we know it

Hailey will get a ring

12/16/2024 – One Week No Weed

Tomorrow is one week no weed

The cravings are starting to breed

Irritability washing over me

Just the smell is good for me

I don't know if that's cheating

But it saves me from reeling

I'm not smoking it, I'm sniffing it

Not forever, just for a little bit

I miss my bong Wall-e

At least I'm not hooked on Molly

10 days sober, but I must admit

It's coming up, but damn, I miss it

11/16/2024 – Something To Pass the Time

I feel like I'm something to pass the time

When he looks away at other women

Even though he has me by his side

A lack of gifts yet to be given

But tales of the ones before

Makes you wonder what made them special

A kind of special I don't seem to have anymore

Maybe I'm not good enough

Maybe I'm not the love they want or need

Maybe I'm just something to pass the time

12/??/2024 — I'm Not Pretty

Maybe I'm not pretty

Or even average at best

Big belly, no baby

My hair is crazy

My ass seems flat

Hair from front to back

From my head to my toes

Coffee and smokes

My teeth turned yellow

Always stressed out

You can smell me out

Scratching myself until I bleed

It's the relief I feel I need

Seasonal Depression – 12/??/2024

November brought the cold

The clouds grey, the feelings' old

Sleeping Beauty, please wake up

So many things you could put in your cup

What about a coffee, maybe some liquor

A quick fix but never a cure

Maybe I need to smoke some weed

Even that doesn't give the boost I need

What if I eat a bunch of junk food

Wont even budge my awful mood

What if I go lie in the shower

I still feel like I'm out of power

If You Think

If you think I'm sitting at home

Crying on the couch all alone

I'm here to tell you I'm not

If you think I'm looking for a man

To walk me through life and hold my hand

I'm here to tell you I'm not

If you think the rules of life

Are equal to the law I should follow

I'm here to tell you I'm not

If you think I need sugar coating

To satisfy your egos' gloating

I'm here to tell you I'm not

If you think I don't know my worth

Even when I'm lying in the dirt

I'm here to tell you I do

I Love the Way You Care

I love the way you care

I love the way we cuddle

I love the way you make me happy

I know my feelings haven't been subtle

A man who takes his time

A man who drives me wild

A man who blows my mind

A man who's good to my child

Someone I want to give my time

You're the drug I'll use for the rest of my life

Thank You for Loving Me Part 2

I love you, thank you for loving me

Mindful of my past

Mindful of my comfort zones

Gentle pushes outside of comfort zones

Surviving a mental health episode

Cuddles and sex

Being there to listen

Showing me, I never asked for too much

Relieving the fear that I would find worse

Fear that you wouldn't be good with the kids

Being good to me and for me

Helping whenever you can

Putting the smile back on my face

Helping me accept weight gain/looks in general

Relieving fear that mental health made me unlovable

Keeping your word with my kids

Caring

Spoiling us

03/14/2025 – Dirty Thirty

She's turning thirty

In ten short days

The death of her twenties

Is coming her way

While she dreads it

She embraces it too

The twenties were rough. What's thirty going to do?

What I'm Looking For

Handsome

Caring yet careless

Smart

Great father

Wonderful smiles

The best cuddles

Awesome hugs

Heart-stopping kisses

Has got that "Ahh"

Great with my kids

Weird Kind of Person

I am a weird kind of person

I am a nice person though

I want to go back

To being the on-call therapist

The one people vented to

Put my mind to the test

Used To Be So Dark

I used to be so dark

Negativity leaking from my lips

Looking for Noah's ark

But the ark was barely a ship

I wanted to be resilient

Until I realized how tiring that was

A new idea that was brilliant

Smooshed Together

My days are smooshed together

Instead of one at a time

Can't tell you what I did

Can't tell you what I've done

Can't tell you why

I'm running from the sun

October Is Here

October is here

The leaves are falling

Who would've thought

Youd still be calling

The colors have changed

But the roots are strong

And before you know it

Winter will be here before long

No Drinks

Welp, no drinks for us tonight

After the battle with my son

I really needed one

I feel like I failed

In The Depths of My Despair

In the depths of my despair

I couldn't find a single care

Didn't even want to wash my hair

I just want to lie over there

So here I am trying to write it out

Trying to figure out what my depression is about

It's coming out like a leaky spout

I wonder if I'm going to wipe out

I Was Hateful

I was hateful

My soul black as night

Don't come near me

Unless you're ready to fight

I'll cut you with my words

I won't need to use my hands

I'll make you feel insecure

It's part of my master plans

And when you've had enough

That's when I start the most

I'm sending out the message

It's not coming via Canada Post

I Was Psychotic

I was psychotic

My negativity won

Ife was so dark

I couldn't see the light

I cried out my heart

That's when I started to heal

Let go of what was

To make room for what is

How You Been Doing

"Hey, how you been doing?"

I've been doing well

So good in fact

I have a story to tell

I found me a wonderful man

In the woods of all places

Turns out he's the man of my dreams

The reason I tied up my laces

My mental health is better

Still not where it should be

At least I'm not paranoid anymore

Wondering who's going to kill me

I'm sorry that you met me

And I didn't stick around

The way you made me feel

It is far from profound

The way I said goodbye

On unforgiving terms

Should've been a sign

I want to avoid you like I avoid germs

I Love My Family

I love my family

The one I've created

Is everything I asked for

And more besides

I'm excited for our future

And all we will accomplish

I hope it continues to be happy

Even on rough days

I Like to Do My Nails

I like to do my nails

And all that entails

Putting on tips

Learning new tricks

Choosing a style

I'll want for a while

A way to relax

When I'm slipping through the cracks

WALL-E The Bong

WALL-E is my bong

We often get along

Unless he gets clogged

Then it tastes like smog

When he's nice and clean

I'm a tokahauntas queen

The prettiest stoner you've seen

I Remember It Well

I remember it well

Stuck in a dark spell

My life a living hell

Living in my own shell

Falling into the same old cycle

Like it's something I disciple

I turned suicidal

Just by being in denial

Things changed on a January day

The cycle was finally going away

New opportunity had a say

All my demons I had to slay

A reason to get and be better

Put the past in the shredder

Accept this newfound pleasure

Write a bunch of thank-you letters

I Didn't See You Coming

I didn't see you coming

You stopped me in my tracks

Ever since we started

I knew there was no going back

Every interaction

Causing chain reactions

Take a step outside my comfort zone

With you, I don't feel like I'm doing it alone

12/31/2025 – I Love Heartbreak in The Winter

I love heartbreak in the winter

The coldness numbs the pain

I thought I had it right for once

But I guess I'll try again

Because I know my love is strong

And I'm worth every second

The kind of love you actually feel

The love of legends

I'll let myself feel

I've let myself fall

I've been stressed out

Now I feel nothing at all

Back to finding me

And shining like a star

Don't care what you think

I'm in the getaway car

It's Too Small for me to be This Sad

"It's too small for me to be this sad"

I said "Depressingly" to my mom

It's almost the smallest I've ever had

Is what I thought to add on

It was alright and sometimes did the job

Other times, it felt a little too soft

Width was okay, the length wasn't long

A new definition of Microsoft

The moans he got were faker than a clone

Carbon copied by me alone

01/13/2026 – The Subject

To be the subject

Of someone's poetry

A pedestal I wish to sit on

01/05/2026 – Her

Moats and boats and trees that are tall

Then I think I'd have it all

I just want to be there with her

The me that felt oh-so-free

Is who I really want to see

Damn, I miss her every single day

I'll take her for a walk and talk

Write her name in yellow chalk

Let her pour love back in me

01/??/2026 – No Exception

Don't tell me to have a good day

After you told me you're done

It's not your concern anymore

You pulled the trigger on that gun

I am no exception to your

"Don't talk to exes" rule

I wasn't good enough to keep

I'm not a damn fool

Everything you lose

Is a step you take

Good luck finding someone

To fuck by the lake

01/10/2026 – I Wake to Heal

I wake every day to heal

From a love I thought was real

How could I be so naive

This loss is something I grieve

I thought I had it right for once

Casual drinks and smoking blunts

Someone to love me through my sick

It was all gone; I didn't heal quick

All you had to do was stay

Eventually, my sickness will go away

I'd be everything you want and more

But you couldn't wait and walked out the door

I was happy for a while there
Wear a dress and wash my hair
Content with life and the way it was
Do my makeup just because

I was happy for a while there
Get a compliment on what I wear
Sleep like a baby through the night
Never heard tell of having a fight

I was happy for a while there
Nothing up to that point could compare
Everything was smooth sailing
Little did I know it was ailing

I was happy for a while there
I thought we were the perfect pair
I thought I found the perfect love
Fitting like a pair of gloves

01/28/2026 – Staring

You've been caught staring at my deck

All can think is what the heck

Is there something that you want to say

Or is it so you can hide away

Part of me thinks I should check on you

The other part says, "What good will that do?"

Do I leave it be, or have something to say

I don't know which one is the right pathway

Mental health takes a toll

With the punches is how I roll

Social anxiety keeps me inside

Depression makes me want to die

Psychosis was a scary time

Did I cross an invisible line

As I tread through these waters

I wonder if I'm going to falter

Will my depression finally win

Drown my sorrows with some gin

Someone, please, take me out

Tired of my head being filled with doubt

02/09/2026 I Scare Them

I scare them away

With three words I say

"I love you"

02/09/2026 – This Thought Knocked, But I Didn't Answer the Door

I should die

I want to drown myself

This thought knocked

But I didn't answer the door

What if he misses me

What if he wants me back

This thought knocked

But I didn't answer the door

I want to send a message

I should check on him

This thought knocked

But I answered the door

I wonder if he's watching for me

Is he looking for me too

This thought knocked

But I didn't answer the door

The thought of him popped up

But I didn't answer the door

02-12-2026 - Dear Reader

Dear reader, thank you

For reading my poems

I wrote most of them at home

The place where I feel somewhat safe

A shelter for a wandering waif

Dear reader, thank you

For holding on

Through your darkest days

Keep being strong

Getting help isn't wrong

Dear reader, thank you

I hope psychosis never hits

But if you find yourself

In a psychotic fit

The doctors are trying to help you

Three Years Writing

Three years of writing

Turns into 6 hours of typing

One exhausted mama

The Doctor

My psychiatrist freaked me out

One day, he was good and kind

Then he would be evil and conniving

I felt like a special circumstance

Like a pawn in his twisted dance

So, I knew I had to play his game

On days he was conniving

He wore a wolf sweater

I knew I had to stay calm

Internally, I was raging

I knew I was sick

But I had to escape

Do what they say

Say what they want to hear

I couldn't write about it then

The nurses read every word

And I felt they were involved

But one day, my plan got me away

I got to go back home

Still suffering through psychosis

But I tried to tell myself I'm fine

In a matter of time, back I go

To a different hospital for help though

That's when I started to heal

Psychosis is scary. Psychosis is real

02/13/2026 – The Heart That Stays

I'm taking a chance

I'm making a change

From an ordinary person

To a new social range

I'm scared as hell

To become truly known

Resonate with people

By the words I own

Mental health

The color Yellow

Smoking weed

And being mellow

Characteristics of me

I want you to remember

Strong and brave

With a heart that stays tender

Love With All I Got

I always love with all I've got

Never pretend to be something I'm not

Almost perfect, but never the one

While it lasts, it's always fun

I come with kids and toys

And all kinds of other joys

All my goods are the gift of God

When I walk past, will you nod?

Here I Go Again

Here I go again

Reading letters I never sent

How much I loved and appreciated you

Now there's nothing left for you

It's been that way

For a while

I noticed the way

I didn't smile

When you walked in

Or entered my mind

Wondering what version

I'd get this time

It had been that way

For an aeon

Just waiting for it

To finally come to light

Questions For My Loved Ones

I asked my friends & family

To answer some questions

They happily obliged

Told me what they see

What reminds them of me

How I make them feel

It sounds like a great deal

To be my friend

And I must agree

To some degree

I felt they were accurate

And true

How wonderful it is

To make people feel great

And a little less blue

That's the power I have over you

This Chapter of Me

This chapter of me

Has come to a close

I'm rising like a phoenix now

A new me to compose

Trust your instinct every day

You know the signs

Don't go astray

Never stop loving

The way that you do

When you are working

On the new you

Keep putting in the work

To get where you want to be

Peaceful, loving, and happily

I Knew to Trust My Gut

My reaction was 100% called for

Your response solidified it

My gut knew something was up

For me to get out fast

Being a bitch saved me

You said you didn't deserve me

The one time you didn't lie

I gave you love, you gave me problems

Fucked my mental health

I knew it wouldn't last

Nothing in common but smoking weed

And being in the woods

That's the first time I realized

This was just to pass the time

The Fire That Burned Inside Me

The fire that burned inside me

Was rapid with realization

I'm not crazy

I'm not dumb

I saw the signs

You told me it was

"Pretty fucking dumb"

That's because I was right

"She's just a friend"

My ass just a friend

"She's married with kids"

Hasn't stopped you before

And look where we are

Once a whore

Always a whore

My Friends Say

My friends say I'm awesome

And fun to be around

I like to think they're right

When my mind is sound

I'm always caring

Sometimes too much

Make you feel loved

With a warm, embracing touch

Lost Myself

I lost myself in the search for love

My environment became negative

It was poisoned by his presence

Rough around the edges

Like trying to love a cactus

Always getting hurt

Never pleasing, always leaving

Feeling on eggshells all the time

Cracks in the ice time after time

Until I broke through

Deep in the water, I did plunge

But I've finally reached the surface

Crawling back onto land

Firmly, I begin to stand

And walk into the woman I am

Candles Flickering

Losing him was dark

But I always saw the light

Little candles flickering

Of what I know was right

Things Are Going to Change

Things are going to change

I'm not going to be the same

I'm still healing from psychosis

I haven't been me in years

Put everyone else above myself

Give in to all my fears

I'm going to love myself

The way I did before

Spoil myself in ways

Nobody thought of before

Buy all my merch

From the Taylor Swift store

Don't try to stop me

It hasn't worked in the past

It makes me happy

Longer than a boy can last

It Gets Easier, Then It Gets Okay, Then It Feels Like Freedom

And I finally feel free

From all the hell you gave me

My life has been very calm

Kids always say I love you mom

Out of nowhere, just because

Back to the way it always was

Spending time doing things

Next, I'll get a family ring

To symbolize my love

I'm the hat, and they're my gloves

Coming Down

I'm coming down from the rush

Knowing it's me that I can trust

I'm going to keep to myself, publish my book

It's going to be a whole new look

I wrote about psychosis

I wrote about my exes

How they made me feel

And I'm still trying to heal

I'm stepping into a new world

Time To Heal Part 2

Time to heal for me

Get my head out of the sand

It's going to take a while to shake it out

But it's always been the plan

Time to heal for me

Do it for the kids

Do everything I can

To screw back on my lid

Time to heal for me

For the adventures that are in store

The richness the future brings

I can't wait to see more

Time to heal for me

To give myself room

Like a lotus flower

I will bloom

So Glad

I am loving

I am kind

I'm so glad

I left you behind

My mind isn't filled

With endless fog

The skies are clear

I love it here

I can't wait

To love again

Someone worthy

Someone kind

Speaks my love language

All the time